Author: Miriam Kensington
ISBN HARDBACK: 978-9916-90-832-7
ISBN PAPERBACK: 978-9916-90-833-4

The Splendor of My Existence

In morning light, I rise anew,
The world unfolds in vibrant hue.
Each breath a gift, each moment bright,
A dance of joy in pure delight.

The whispers of the gentle breeze,
Speak tales of wonder 'neath the trees.
As nature sings its sweet refrain,
I feel the pulse of life sustain.

With every step, a path I trace,
In this grand journey, I find grace.
The mountains high, the rivers deep,
In splendor's arms, my spirit leaps.

With heart wide open, I embrace,
The beauty found in every place.
In love and laughter, I invest,
In the splendor of my existence, blessed.

Immensity Wrapped in Grace

Beneath the stars, a sky so wide,
I find my thoughts like waves abide.
The cosmos hums a timeless tune,
In silence deep, I touch the moon.

Each heartbeat echoes through the vast,
A memory of futures past.
In every moment, stillness reigns,
Where hope and dreams break all the chains.

The ocean's depth, the mountains high,
Reflect the grace where spirits fly.
In nature's arms, I seek my place,
An endless dance, an endless space.

As day and night in harmony blend,
I find the light that dreams transcend.
With every breath, I feel embraced,
In this immensity wrapped in grace.

Ascending the Stairs of Ambition

Each step I take, a dream unfolds,
The heights of hope, a story told.
With every rise, my heart ignites,
Ambition's fire, shining bright.

Challenges come, but so do gains,
Hard work's path through joys and pains.
I reach for stars, my spirit soars,
Each stair I climb, it opens doors.

Ripples of My Resolve

In still waters, my thoughts take flight,
Ripples spread with dreams in sight.
Each drop of courage starts to weave,
The fabric of what I believe.

Waves may crash, but I stand strong,
With every setback, I belong.
My spirit flows with the tide's embrace,
Rippling onward, I find my place.

The Canvas of My Aspirations

A canvas blank, my heart's delight,
Colors splash in morning light.
Brush strokes dance, a vivid tale,
Aspirations launch, I will not fail.

Each hue a hope, each line a plan,
Creating dreams as only I can.
With patience, I'll craft my design,
The masterpiece of this life of mine.

Unfolding like a Lotus

From murky depths, I find my way,
Unfolding petals greet the day.
In silent grace, I venture forth,
A lotus blooms, proving worth.

Each barrier faced, a step to grow,
Emerging stronger, bending low.
In water's embrace, I rise and shine,
A symbol of hope, forever divine.

Symphony of Immense Thoughts

In the quiet of the night, they sing,
Whispers of wisdom, their voices ring.
Echoes of dreams from afar,
Guiding the lost like a shining star.

Thoughts like rivers, flowing deep,
In their currents, secrets keep.
Melodies born from ages past,
A symphony of shadows cast.

Each note a journey, each pause a sigh,
Moments that linger, where we fly.
Reverberating through the soul,
Awakening visions that make us whole.

Gather them close, let them unfold,
Tales of wonder yet to be told.
In this grand chorus, we find our place,
Joining the dance of the cosmic grace.

Radiating Greatness

From the depths of the heart, a spark ignites,
Illuminating paths, reaching new heights.
With every step, the courage grows,
A beacon of strength that forever glows.

In whispers of hope, we find our power,
As the sun ascends in the morning hour.
Together we rise, relentless and free,
Bound by the magic of unity.

Glimmers of grace in every smile,
Reflecting the essence of life's great trial.
As stars align in the vast expanse,
We embrace our journey, a sacred dance.

Radiating greatness wherever we go,
With every challenge, our spirits grow.
In the tapestry woven by fate's design,
We shine as one, distinctly divine.

Fortitude in Epics

Boldly we stand on the edge of time,
Carving our stories, sublime in rhyme.
Through battles fought and tears we shed,
Fortitude rises, where angels tread.

Legends are born in the heat of strife,
In the crucible of pain, we find our life.
Echoes of valor in every heart,
Guiding the brave who dare to start.

With every chapter, we learn to thrive,
Embracing the struggle that keeps us alive.
In the pages of history, we lay our claim,
Forever entwined in the heart of the flame.

Together we write our tales of might,
In the fading glow of the evening light.
Fortitude whispers in every breath,
A promise of life that conquers death.

The Embrace of the Infinite

In the silence of the cosmos so wide,
We find our fear and let it subside.
Cradled in stardust, gently we sway,
Lost in the magic, night turns to day.

Every heartbeat echoes with grace,
Connecting the threads of time and space.
In the embrace of the infinite sky,
We soar with dreams that never die.

A dance of the galaxies, tender and bold,
Whispers of secrets waiting to be told.
As we reach for the stars, hand in hand,
Together as one, forever we stand.

The universe hums a familiar song,
Inviting our spirits, where we belong.
In unity found, we begin to see,
The endless embrace that sets us free.

Beyond the Reach of Doubt

In shadows deep, where hopes reside,
A whisper calls, a heart's own guide.
Through trials fierce, we forge our way,
Embracing dawn, we greet the day.

With every step, the fear unwinds,
A courage found in seeking minds.
Beyond the veil, the light breaks through,
A world reborn, anew, so true.

A Canvas of My Infinity

Brush strokes dance across the page,
Colors blend, they set the stage.
Imagination takes its flight,
In vast expanse, I chase the light.

Each dream a hue, each thought a line,
In this creation, my soul will shine.
A canvas wide, where visions play,
In endless beauty, I'll find my way.

Emblazoned in Radiance

Stars ignite the velvet sky,
Each twinkle whispers, hearts comply.
In golden gleams, our spirits soar,
Together we can dream once more.

With every dawn, the colors bloom,
Life's symphony dispels the gloom.
Emblazoned bright, our hopes align,
In radiant light, our love will shine.

My Boundless Horizon

Across the waves, the horizon calls,
A promise waits as daylight falls.
With dreams in tow, I sail the seas,
Towards the future, wild and free.

Mountains loom where skies embrace,
A path awaits, my fears will face.
In every step, new worlds unfold,
My boundless journey, brave and bold.

The Towering Essence

In shadows tall, the towers rise,
Their stories etched in weary sighs.
Each brick a tale of time gone past,
A whispering breath that seems to last.

The winds will dance through halls of stone,
With secrets kept, yet never known.
Their essence strong, they touch the sky,
In silence, they will always lie.

Heart of a Giant

Beneath the stars, a heartbeat grows,
A gentle pulse that nature knows.
It echoes dreams of hopes untold,
In whispers soft, both brave and bold.

With every thump to earth it sends,
A rhythm where the river bends.
The giant's heart, both fierce and wide,
Contains the strength of time and tide.

The Universe in My Eyes

Within my gaze, the cosmos swirls,
In vibrant hues, a dance unfurls.
Galaxies spin in gentle grace,
Each spark a story, a lost embrace.

I see the sun as it ignites,
The moon's soft glow on chilly nights.
Stars twinkle like forgotten dreams,
Reflecting all that life redeems.

Defying the Ordinary

In mundane days, a spark ignites,
A chance encounter, unexpected sights.
The gray gives way to vivid strokes,
As laughter breaks, the silence chokes.

We leap from norms, take daring flight,
To find the glow in black and white.
With open hearts, the brave explore,
And in the chaos, we find our core.

Chords of Empowerment

In the melody of courage, I rise,
Each note a promise, fierce and wise.
With every strum, I break the chains,
Harmonies of strength in joyful refrains.

Voices united, we sing as one,
Echoes of battles fought and won.
The rhythm pulses, a heart so bold,
In these chords, my story is told.

Charting My Own Universe

Stars align in patterns I create,
In the canvas of my dreams, I paint my fate.
Galaxies spin with each decision,
Navigating through my own vision.

With constellations guiding my way,
I forge my path, come what may.
Infinite space, no limits confine,
In this universe, I brightly shine.

The Thrill of Eclipsing Limits

Like shadows crossing the light of day,
I dare to challenge, to break away.
With every step, I defy the norm,
Eclipsing limits, I rise, transform.

A dance of freedom, fierce and bold,
In this moment, my spirit unfolds.
No barriers strong enough to bind,
For in my heart, true strength I find.

A Crown of Stars

Adorned with dreams, I wear my crown,
Each star a victory, a symbol renowned.
Radiant glimmers, I hold them tight,
Guiding my journey, through darkest night.

With every twinkle, a tale is spun,
A map of the battles I have won.
In the galaxy of my own design,
I reign with grace, my spirit divine.

The Colossus in the Mirror

In the glass, a giant stands,
Casting dreams with mighty hands.
Reflections ripple, shadows play,
A silent strength that lights the way.

Each crack and line, a tale to tell,
Of silent battles fought so well.
Through every flaw, a story weaves,
The heart that dares, and never grieves.

With every gaze, resilience grows,
The fiercest fire deep below.
A colossus bold, unbowed, upright,
Shining fierce in the darkest night.

Embrace the strength, refuse to flee,
In the mirror, find the real me.
For in this frame, no fear shall dwell,
A titan's heart, I know so well.

A Heart Swelling with Light

A flicker bright within my chest,
An ember warm, a gentle guest.
It whispers soft, ignites the air,
The joy that dances everywhere.

With every beat, the world ignites,
A symphony of endless nights.
In twilight's glow, I'm lifted high,
A heart that swells beneath the sky.

Each laugh, each tear, a spark within,
Together weave the threads of kin.
From darkness deep to skies of blue,
This light is forged from me and you.

Let kindness guide, let mercy reign,
In the heart's swell, there's no more pain.
Together we shine, a brilliant sight,
A world transformed by love and light.

Brimming with Prominence

In every step, a tale unfolds,
A journey rich, a heart of gold.
With every shout, let voices rise,
Brimming bright under endless skies.

Each moment lived, a chance to grow,
A river's flow, a steady show.
Through valleys deep, to peaks so high,
The spirit leaps and learns to fly.

Stand tall and proud, let shadows fade,
In every glance, a grand parade.
The promise lives in every dream,
In vibrant hues, life finds its theme.

With open arms, embrace the grace,
In every heart, there's a sacred space.
Brimming with strength, together we shine,
Prominence found in the divine.

Lighthouse of My Abilities

In stormy seas, I find my way,
A lighthouse bright, a guiding ray.
With beams of hope, I chart the night,
My spirit lifts, a soaring flight.

Each wave that crashes, a chance to rise,
Strength resides within, never shies.
The beacon calls, a promise near,
In every challenge, I persevere.

Rock and tide, they shape my form,
Crafting courage, weathering storm.
With every triumph, I ignite,
A lighthouse built on inner light.

So here I stand, unwavering ground,
In my abilities, purpose found.
Guiding others to shores of peace,
In this vast sea, I find my lease.

Radiance of a Thousand Suns

In the dawn's early light, we rise,
Cascading warmth across the skies.
A thousand suns in our embrace,
Illuminating every face.

Golden rays that softly dance,
Whispering hope in every glance.
With hearts ablaze and spirits free,
We shine as bright as we can be.

From mountain peaks to ocean's shore,
Our radiance opens every door.
Together we weave a tapestry,
Of dreams and light, a symphony.

With courage fierce and passions bold,
We share our stories, dreams untold.
In unity, let our spirits run,
A radiant force, a thousand suns.

Expanding Horizons

Beyond the mountains, the seas so wide,
We seek the path, with hearts as guides.
Each step unfolds a brand new view,
Expanding horizons, bright and true.

The world is vast, its wonders call,
In every corner, we can have it all.
Through valleys deep and skies so clear,
We find our purpose, drawing near.

With open minds and willing hearts,
We navigate where adventure starts.
In every challenge, growth we find,
Expanding horizons, soul unconfined.

Let dreams ignite, let passions soar,
A journey awaits, forever more.
Together we chase the sunlit skies,
In this great expanse, our spirits rise.

The Symphony of Strength

In the quiet moments, strength resides,
A symphony where courage abides.
With every heartbeat, a note we find,
Resilient spirits, eternally aligned.

From whispered wounds to battles fought,
In unity, our lessons taught.
A melody crafted through pain and grace,
The symphony of strength we embrace.

With voices rising, we stand as one,
Harmony flows like the setting sun.
Each challenge faced, a song to sing,
Together we rise, empowered in spring.

Let the notes of hope fill the air,
A testament to the strength we share.
In every struggle, a chorus strong,
The symphony of strength carries on.

Embracing the Vastness Within

In the silence of the night, we find,
A vast expanse within the mind.
Where dreams take flight and shadows play,
Embracing the vastness, come what may.

Through every tear and joyous smile,
We journey deep, mile by mile.
In the depths of soul, we explore,
A universe waiting to be more.

With open arms, we greet our fears,
Transforming doubts into shining spheres.
For in the depths of who we are,
Lies the potential to reach the stars.

So let us breathe, let our spirits sing,
Embracing the vastness, life's offering.
With every heartbeat, let wonders unfold,
In the vastness within, we are consoled.

Shattering Ceilings with Dreams

With a whisper, we rise high,
Breaking limits, reaching the sky.
Hope ignites in every heart,
From fragments, we will not part.

Voices merging, a fervent song,
In this struggle, we all belong.
Hands together, strong and bold,
The stories of the brave unfold.

Every setback fuels our fire,
Dreams can lift us ever higher.
In this vision, we unite,
Chasing futures, full of light.

The glass may crack; we won't fall,
Together, we will stand tall.
Shattering ceilings, we'll convene,
A force of dreams, fierce and keen.

Anchored in Power

Deep roots rise from fertile ground,
In the silence, strength is found.
With each challenge, we grow more,
Anchored in power, we will soar.

Resilience flows through our veins,
Turning losses into gains.
In unity, our spirits beam,
Together, we turn every dream.

Storms may rage, winds may howl,
But we stand firm, we will not cowl.
The heartbeat echoes, loud and true,
Anchored in power, we break through.

With courage as our guiding light,
We'll embrace the darkest night.
Brave and bold, we march in line,
Anchored in power, we will shine.

Garden of My Giants

In the soil where dreams arise,
Giants stand beneath the skies.
Roots entwined, their stories grow,
In this garden, planted slow.

Each tale whispers through the trees,
Strength and wisdom in the breeze.
From the shadows, they have bloomed,
In their presence, I am groomed.

Fruits of labor, sweet and rare,
Nurtured with a loving care.
In the sunlight, they ignite,
Garden of giants, pure delight.

With every step, I walk their path,
Learning courage, sharing laughs.
In their shade, my heart shall dwell,
In this garden, all is well.

Navigating through the Vast Unseen

Stars above guide my way,
In the night, they gently sway.
Through the shadows, I will roam,
Finding courage, finding home.

Currents pull, and waves may crash,
But I hold fast, I will not dash.
In the depth, I seek the light,
Navigating through the night.

Every twist, a new delight,
Chasing dreams with all my might.
In the silence, I will find,
Strength and peace within my mind.

Though the path may feel unknown,
Every step, I claim my own.
In this journey, I begin,
Navigating through the vast unseen.

Harboring Greatness

In the depths of quiet seas,
Greatness waits, a whispered breeze.
Anchored deep in heart and soul,
Yearning dreams that make us whole.

Tides of doubt may pull and sway,
But steadfast hearts will find their way.
With each wave that crashes down,
Rise anew, wear strength like crown.

Stars above, a guiding light,
They spark the courage to ignite.
In every storm, we hold our ground,
For within, our truth is found.

My Spirit, Unshackled

Wings unfurl beneath the sky,
As chains of old begin to die.
With each breath, I claim my space,
Unshackled now, I find my pace.

Voices whisper soft and clear,
The call of dreams, I hold so dear.
No longer bound by fear's embrace,
I dance through life, a wild grace.

The heart ignites like fires bright,
Guided forth by purest light.
In freedom's song, I learn to soar,
My spirit free, forevermore.

A Colossal Whisper

In the silence, bold and deep,
A whisper stirs from dreams we keep.
It carries tales from far and wide,
Of hopes and fears we cannot hide.

Mountains rise from voices strong,
In shadows cast, we find our song.
A colossal roar, yet soft as sighs,
It lingers long beneath the skies.

With every heartbeat's rhythmic pulse,
We weave a truth that won't convulse.
In whispers grand, our spirits weave,
A tapestry of hope, believe.

Dreams That Touch the Stars

With every glance at night's embrace,
Dreams ignite in boundless space.
They shimmer bright, like lanterns glow,
Inviting us to dance and flow.

In every wish, a beacon shines,
A path of light, where spirit twines.
To touch the stars, we reach with care,
For dreams fulfill the open air.

Whispers linger in the night,
Encouraging hearts to take flight.
For in our dreams, we find our way,
To realms where magic leads the day.

The Dance of My Shadow

In the fading light I see,
My shadow sways and twirls free,
It leaps with grace upon the ground,
A silent dance, no one around.

Underneath the moon's soft glow,
My shadow moves, a gentle flow,
It whispers secrets in the night,
In every step, pure delight.

With every breeze, it takes a chance,
It leads me on in a moonlit dance,
Together we find our way anew,
In shadows deep, where dreams come true.

Blooming Beyond the Horizon

Petals burst in morning's light,
Colors spill, a pure delight,
Whispers of the dawn's embrace,
Beauty blooms in every space.

Fields of gold beneath the sky,
Where soft winds and blossoms lie,
Nature sings in perfect rhyme,
A chorus sweet, transcending time.

Beyond the hills, where dreams arise,
Hope and joy in vast supplies,
A garden grows, both wild and free,
Awakening the heart to see.

Towers of Determination

Brick by brick, we build our dreams,
Unyielding strength, or so it seems,
With every trial that we face,
We rise again, we find our place.

High above, the towers gleam,
Each one born from steadfast dream,
Through storms and strife, we hold our ground,
In unity, our souls are bound.

With every stone, a story told,
Of courage fierce and spirits bold,
Together we stand, hand in hand,
In towers tall, we make our stand.

Embracing the Sky

Wings outstretched, I take the flight,
Embracing dawn, the world so bright,
With open arms, I reach for dreams,
In endless blue, my spirit beams.

Clouds beneath, I soar and glide,
With every heartbeat, I confide,
The whispers of the winds so high,
In their embrace, I learn to fly.

The sun kisses my eager face,
In every journey, find my place,
With skies so vast, I feel alive,
In every breath, my hopes will thrive.

The Roar of My Spirit

In the quiet, whispers rise,
Echoes of strength in my sighs.
Mountains tremble, skies ignite,
A fire within, a fearless fight.

With every heartbeat, thunder calls,
Breaking chains, tearing down walls.
I'll stand tall, with unwavering force,
Embracing the path, my true course.

Resilience flows through my veins,
Weathering storms, dancing in rains.
The roar of my spirit, wild and free,
Guides me forward, eternally.

In the depths of night, stars will gleam,
I forge ahead, chasing a dream.
With each roar, my spirit will rise,
Transcending limits, embracing the skies.

A Cloud of Possibilities

Drifting softly, a whisper floats,
Carrying dreams on gentle notes.
Winds of change, a sweet caress,
In this moment, I find my quest.

Colors blend in twilight's gleam,
Crafting futures from each dream.
A canvas vast, horizons expand,
Infinite choices at my command.

With every heartbeat, hope takes flight,
Guided by stars in the night.
A cloud of possibilities, so near,
Inviting me to conquer my fear.

In the dance of life, I embrace the whim,
Chasing dreams, my spirit won't dim.
In this cloud, my heart will soar,
Opening doors to what's in store.

The Pulse of Greatness

Deep within, a rhythm beats,
Echoes of greatness, life's sweet feats.
In every challenge, strength reveals,
The pulse within, it fiercely feels.

Mountains rise, shadows fall,
In this journey, I hear the call.
Each step forward, courage is born,
A testament to the dreams I've worn.

With every heartbeat, whispers grow,
Knowledge gained, wisdom to show.
The pulse of greatness surges on,
Inspiring hearts, from dusk till dawn.

So I rise, unyielding and bold,
Writing my story, a tale to be told.
The pulse of greatness, forever mine,
In this moment, I will shine.

Sails of an Unbroken Dream

In the harbor of hope, I set my course,
With sails wide open, powered by force.
Navigating tides, both rough and calm,
An unbroken dream, my heart's sweet balm.

Waves crashing, a symphony plays,
Guiding my spirit through murky bays.
With the stars as my guide, I roam,
An endless voyage, far from home.

The winds whisper secrets of yore,
Each gust ignites a longing for more.
Sails of determination, lifting high,
Chasing horizons beneath vast sky.

So I journey on, through storm and sun,
With each new dawn, my heart's begun.
Sails of an unbroken dream, it seems,
I sail forever, through boundless dreams.

The Height of My Dreams

I reach for the stars, so bright,
With hopes that soar like kites in flight.
Each vision glimmers, bold and true,
In the depths of night, I find my cue.

Through valleys dark, I tread with care,
The whispering winds, they guide my prayer.
In the height of dreams, I chase the light,
With every heartbeat, I will ignite.

No fear can bind my soaring heart,
In the tapestry of life, I play my part.
Infinite skies, my spirit free,
Embracing all that's yet to be.

So watch me rise, with unwavering grace,
In the height of dreams, I find my place.
Together with the dawn, I ascend,
To the heights of dreams that never end.

Vastness Beneath My Skin

Beneath the surface, a world untold,
A universe of secrets, rich and bold.
Each pulse, a story, whispered low,
The vastness within starts to glow.

The rivers of thought, they intertwine,
Mapping the depths, like roots of a vine.
In every heartbeat, a voyage awaits,
The expanse of being reverberates.

Mountains of dreams, valleys of pain,
Through storms of sorrow, I shall remain.
Embracing the feelings, the wildest spin,
Finding the vastness beneath my skin.

In every struggle, strength is born,
A tapestry woven from dusk till dawn.
The canvas of life, intricately designs,
The vastness beneath, it forever shines.

Spirit of the Colossus

With iron resolve, I stand so tall,
A spirit ignited, I shall not fall.
The weight of giants rests in my soul,
In the face of storms, I stay whole.

Each challenge faced, a step I take,
With fervor and fire, I shall not break.
The echoes of history guide my way,
In the spirit of the Colossus, I sway.

Defying the odds, I rise above,
Fueled by the strength of those I love.
In shadows cast by giants long gone,
The spirit of the Colossus, I draw upon.

With every heartbeat, power flows,
A testament to the strength that grows.
I stand unyielding, a beacon bright,
In the spirit of the Colossus, I find my might.

Ascending Heights of Confidence

With wings of hope, I take to the sky,
Embracing the chances, I spread my high.
Each step a triumph, I claim my space,
Ascending heights with unwavering grace.

The echoes of doubt may try to bind,
But I cast them off, no fear in mind.
With every ascent, new vistas appear,
In heights of confidence, I persevere.

The clouds may swirl, the winds may howl,
Yet I remain steady, I shall not cowl.
Each moment a lesson, every breath a gift,
In the realm of confidence, my spirit lifts.

So I soar on dreams, a thrilling dance,
Grasping the world with heart and chance.
Ascending to heights, I fear no fall,
With confidence flowing, I shall have it all.

Embracing My Colossal Heart

In the depths of my soul's embrace,
A love so vast, it knows no space.
Waves of warmth crash on the shore,
My heart beats loud, yearning for more.

Gentle whispers float on the breeze,
Carrying hopes, bringing me ease.
With every thump, a story unfolds,
In this rhythm, my truth beholds.

Through valleys low and mountains high,
I rise with grace, I learn to fly.
My colossal heart, a beacon bright,
Guiding my way through day and night.

So I stand tall, unafraid to feel,
With open arms, my wounds will heal.
Embracing love, both wide and deep,
In this great heart, my dreams I'll keep.

Echoes of Immensity

The mountains echo, whispers clear,
Voices of ages, drawing near.
In every shadow, secrets creep,
Tales of the vastness, softly seep.

The winds sing songs of ancient lore,
Calling out from the ocean's core.
Ripples of time in the moonlight's sway,
Dancing through night, leading the way.

Stars above twinkle with pride,
In the realm of dreams where spirits glide.
Their light, a promise that never fades,
In the heart of darkness, hope invades.

Echoes, they linger, a timeless song,
Uniting us all, where we belong.
In this vast expanse, together we roam,
Finding our place, forever our home.

Unfurling My Titan Wings

With each dawn, a fire ignites,
Yearning to soar, chasing heights.
Wings of strength, unfurl with grace,
Taking flight in this sacred space.

Mountains bow to my fierce ascent,
Whispers of winds, a calming scent.
Every flap, a dance with the sky,
Embracing freedom, learning to fly.

Through clouds I weave, a tapestry grand,
Tracing the contours of this wild land.
The world below, a canvas wide,
As I glide on waves of pride.

Unfurling my wings, a bold decree,
In the vastness, just being me.
No more chains, no more restraint,
In this moment, my heart, it paints.

Roaring with the Cosmos

In the belly of night, stars ignite,
Cosmic rhythms, a fierce delight.
The universe churns, a heartbeat clear,
Roaring with passion, far and near.

Galaxies swirl, a vivid dance,
Inviting souls to take their chance.
With each pulse, the cosmos sings,
Awakening dreams that soar on wings.

An orchestra plays in the silent dark,
Echoes of life, a luminous spark.
With each roar, a story unfolds,
Of love, of loss, of destinies told.

So I join in, my voice a part,
Roaring with the cosmos, a beating heart.
Together we rise, in unity strong,
In this celestial dance, we all belong.

Unraveled by My Brilliance

In whispers of the night sky, I gleam,
Woven threads of dreams burst at the seam.
Each spark ignites a path, unconfined,
With every step, my brilliance is defined.

Through trials faced, I wear my crown,
The weight of doubts cannot pull me down.
A tapestry of resilience I weave,
In my heart's fire, I eternally believe.

When shadows loom and darkness creeps,
My spirit rises, the tempest leaps.
With light as my guide, I forge ahead,
Unraveled truths dance, where others dread.

So let the world witness my grace,
As I embrace my rightful place.
With every heartbeat, I shall remind,
The brilliance within cannot be confined.

Statue of My Ambitions

Carved from dreams in a stone so rare,
Each ambition molded with utmost care.
I stand firm, a vision bold and bright,
Radiating hope in the soft moonlight.

My gaze fixed on the horizon afar,
Guided gently by my own north star.
With every chisel, my essence grows,
In the heart of stone, my ambition flows.

Though storms may pound, and shadows creep,
My spirit stands strong, my roots run deep.
A testament to what I strive to be,
A statue alive, forever free.

Each day I rise, sculpted by my hand,
In a world of chaos, I make a stand.
For in the silence, my strength is drawn,
A statue of ambitions, forever dawn.

Journey Through Majestic Terrain

A path unfolds through valleys deep,
Where mountains cradle secrets they keep.
With every turn, the earth whispers tales,
Of ancient paths and shipwrecked sails.

The sun dips low, casting golden light,
Illuminating dreams throughout the night.
Each step a heartbeat in nature's song,
As I wander free where I belong.

Rivers sing, carrying stories wide,
In their embrace, I find my guide.
Through forests dense and skies so vast,
The journey beckons, a spell cast.

Majestic views, painting skies of blue,
Open my heart to horizons new.
In this grand dance with the world I roam,
I find in each step, a piece of home.

Voice of the Monument

In silence stood, a witness to years,
I echo the laughter, the sorrows, the tears.
A voice of the past, carved in stone,
Whispering secrets in a world overgrown.

Each crack tells a story of time long gone,
Of heroes and spirits who gracefully shone.
With open arms, I greet the tales,
Of love and of hope that forever prevails.

Though ages shift like the sands in the breeze,
In the heart of my stillness, truths find their ease.
I stand as a guide through the shadows of time,
A monument's voice, in rhythm and rhyme.

Let me be heard, as the moments unwind,
In the fabric of history, connections bind.
For in every echo, the past remains near,
The voice of the monument, eternally clear.

Walking in Vastness

Beneath the sky so wide and blue,
I wander forth, my dreams in view.
Mountains call with ancient pride,
In the vastness, I confide.

The breeze whispers tales of old,
As I walk where paths unfold.
Every step, a heartbeat's song,
Nature's arms, where I belong.

Oceans stretch to meet the light,
Waves embrace the quiet night.
In solitude, I find my grace,
In vastness, I enjoy my space.

Stars appear, a glittered map,
Guiding me with a gentle tap.
I walk beneath this endless dome,
In the vastness, I find home.

Mask of the Majestic

In halls of stone, the echoes breathe,
Whispers weave a tale beneath.
Majestic masks, a silent show,
Guarding secrets we long to know.

Golden eyes in shadows gleam,
Life unfolds like a timeless dream.
Each facade a story held,
In their presence, hearts are compelled.

Through vibrant halls, I make my way,
Captivated by the play.
Fingers trace the carved designs,
In every line, a world aligns.

Beneath the grandeur, truths appear,
Each mask reflects a hidden fear.
Yet courage blooms in each embrace,
In silent strength, I find my place.

Every Step a Statement

With every footfall on the ground,
A voice emerges, clear and sound.
Paths untraveled, dreams ignite,
Every step a spark of light.

Mountains rise and valleys bend,
Courage grows, no need to pretend.
With open heart, I claim my space,
Every move, a bold embrace.

In the rhythm, I find my beat,
With confidence, I greet defeat.
Strength unfolds with each new day,
Every step a chance to sway.

As shadows fade with morning's glow,
I walk the path, my spirit grows.
Every step, my story told,
With every stride, I break the mold.

Rhapsody of Unbound Courage

In the heart where fear resides,
A melody of strength abides.
Courage sings, a soaring tune,
A rhapsody beneath the moon.

Through the storms, my spirit thrives,
Dancing flames where courage strives.
Each note resonates with power,
In every breath, I find my flower.

With echoes strong, the past rewrites,
Unbound by chains, I reach new heights.
In the symphony of the brave,
I learn the art of how to save.

Each triumph woven in the song,
In unity, we all belong.
Together we rise, hand in hand,
In this brave world, we take our stand.

The Air Beneath My Wings

With gentle whispers of the breeze,
I rise above the weight of doubt.
Each feathered hope, a soft release,
In faith, I learn what life's about.

The sun ignites my fears to flight,
As shadows fade, I find my way.
Embracing dreams that feel so right,
I soar above the fray each day.

Through lofty heights, I see the world,
My spirit dances, wild and free.
In every moment, joy unfurled,
The air beneath supports me, see.

A journey paved with trust and grace,
As winds of change are my delight.
I'll chase the clouds, my fears erase,
With wings of hope, I take my flight.

The Fire of Self-Belief

A flicker sparks within my core,
It blazes bright, it fuels my soul.
With every doubt, I crave for more,
This inner flame makes me feel whole.

I nurture it with care and pride,
Each challenge met ignites the spark.
Through darkest times, I will not hide,
The fire glows, a guiding mark.

Resilience forged with every test,
Through storms and trials, I remain.
With self-belief, I stand my best,
The flame within will break the chain.

My spirit burns with fierce intent,
A beacon strong through night and day.
With every step, my heart's content,
The fire of self-belief will stay.

A Beacon Through the Storm

When thunder roars and winds arise,
A light appears to guide my way.
It shimmers bright, a safe surprise,
A beacon strong, it won't betray.

Through tempest's rage and darkened skies,
I hold this light within my heart.
With every wave that tries to rise,
I feel the strength of a new start.

The storm can come, but I won't break,
This light will shine, a steadfast friend.
Through trials harsh, for hope's own sake,
A beacon bright, my soul will fend.

In shadows deep, this truth I find,
With courage fierce, I'll see it through.
A beacon's glow, forever kind,
Through every storm, I'll start anew.

The Garden of My Giants

In fertile soil, their roots run deep,
With wisdom flourished through the years.
Their towering forms, a watch I keep,
In awe, I face my hopes and fears.

Each story shared, a seed bestowed,
In laughter's shade, I find my way.
With nurturing hands, their love flowed,
In this garden, dreams bloom and sway.

The giants stand, their shadows cast,
A testament to strength divine.
Through storms that pass and shadows vast,
Their legacy in me will shine.

With every blossom, I aspire,
To grow and blossom in their light.
In this vast garden, spirits higher,
My giants' love will guide my flight.

Embracing My Inner Atlas

In shadows deep, I seek the light,
Maps unfold, guiding me through night.
Each step a journey, paths unknown,
With every heartbeat, I am grown.

Mountains whisper secrets true,
Oceans sing in colors blue.
The compass spins, my heart ignites,
A world within, my soul takes flights.

Through valleys low and peaks so high,
I walk with dreams that fill the sky.
Embracing all, I stand and sway,
My inner atlas leads the way.

With open arms, I greet the vast,
A tapestry of futures cast.
In every twist, in every turn,
The fire of exploration burns.

Larger Than the Horizon

Beyond the edge where sun meets sea,
Infinite dreams call out to me.
Each wave that breaks, a story told,
In the embrace of blue and gold.

The sky expands, horizons blend,
Through whispered winds, my spirit bends.
Mountains rise in the fading light,
Bigger dreams take off in flight.

Stars align in a cosmic dance,
I find my faith, I take a chance.
With every step, my heart expands,
Larger dreams await my hands.

A canvas vast, yet so close still,
I paint my world with iron will.
With courage strong, I chase the dawn,
In every heartbeat, I feel drawn.

The Landscape of My Spirit

In quiet woods, my thoughts take flight,
Each rustling leaf, a spark of light.
The rivers flow with tales untold,
The landscape blooms, both fierce and bold.

Mountains echo, wisdom shared,
In nature's arms, I am ensnared.
The valleys cradle dreams to grow,
Beneath the stars, my spirit glows.

In the wild, I find my breath,
Among the trees, I conquer death.
The earth beneath, a sacred ground,
In every heartbeat, peace is found.

The horizons stretch, a call to roam,
In every step, I carve my home.
The landscape of my spirit thrives,
Through art and nature, my soul strives.

Boundaries Met in Flourish

In the garden, colors play,
Boundaries fade with each new day.
Roots dig deep, entwine and grow,
Life abundant, in joy they sow.

Petals open, reaching wide,
In every heart, a dream inside.
Where lines dissolve and merge as one,
The dance of life has just begun.

Seasons change, yet still we bloom,
In every shadow, dispel the gloom.
Together we create and weave,
In every moment, we believe.

With every breath, we push the past,
Boundaries break, our spirits cast.
In unity, we find our way,
Flourishing bright, come what may.

Elevating the Ordinary

In the stillness of dawn's gentle light,
Whispers of promise take to flight.
Moments cherished, simple and clear,
Transform the mundane into something dear.

A cup of tea, steam swirling high,
Painting warmth beneath the sky.
Soft laughter shared, a fleeting glance,
In these fragments, life's sweet dance.

The rustle of leaves, a child's soft sigh,
Ordinary things beckon us nigh.
Every heartbeat, every sigh,
Elevates the simple, makes spirits fly.

So pause awhile, let wonder ignite,
In everyday magic, we find our light.

The Power of the Unseen

Beneath the surface, where shadows creep,
Lies a force that awakens from sleep.
Silent strength, a pulse so profound,
In quiet moments, true power is found.

The warmth of kindness, a hand we lend,
Echoes of love that never end.
Invisible threads weave our fate,
Binding us closer, never too late.

Dreams take flight on wings of grace,
Unseen currents, gently embrace.
In the heart's whisper, in softest sigh,
Lives the power that lifts us high.

So trust in the unseen, the spirit's decree,
For in the hidden, we are truly free.

Echoes of My Boundless Being

In the mirror of the stars, I see my soul,
Reflections of dreams that make me whole.
Each heartbeat whispers a truth so clear,
Echoes of purpose, I hold dear.

The tapestry of thoughts, both loud and shy,
Woven together, they stretch the sky.
In solitude's arms, I rise and sing,
A chorus of being, my spirit takes wing.

Through valleys deep and mountains high,
I chase the echoes that never die.
A symphony born from life's grand design,
In every note, my essence align.

So let the echoes of my boundless frame
Resound through the cosmos, in love's sweet name.

The Stature of My Resolve

In the depths of struggle, my spirit stands tall,
Carved from the grit that defies the fall.
Upon the mountains of challenge I tread,
With each step forward, my fears I shed.

The fire within burns fierce and bright,
Guiding me through the darkest night.
With courage as armor, I face the storm,
In the chaos, I find my form.

Lessons learned from the trials faced,
In the forge of will, I am embraced.
Each setback a stone, each triumph a song,
Strengthened by passion that keeps me strong.

So let the world witness my steadfast aim,
The stature of my resolve, a burning flame.

The Magnitude of My Dreams

In the quiet of the night, they gleam,
Whispers of hope, the echo of a dream.
Stars align in the vast, dark skies,
Carving paths where my spirit flies.

Each vision strong, a flicker of light,
Guiding me through the shadows of night.
With courage and grace, I will pursue,
The heights of joy in all I do.

Brick by brick, I build my way,
A fortress of dreams that will not sway.
With every heartbeat, the fire ignites,
Fueling the passion that burns so bright.

So here I stand, with open heart,
Ready to play an ambitious part.
The magnitude of dreams, so vast and wide,
In every moment, they shall abide.

Immense in Every Breath

Inhale the power, exhale the doubt,
Life unfolds, with joy throughout.
Each breath a canvas, wide and deep,
Painting the moments, vivid and steep.

The rhythm of life, a gentle tide,
Carrying hopes where dreams reside.
With every gasp, a story to tell,
Immense in beauty, as all is well.

Feel the pulse of the world so near,
The whispers of love, the laughter, the cheer.
In every heartbeat, a sacred song,
Resonating where we all belong.

So let us cherish the air we breathe,
In the embrace of life, we shall believe.
Immense in every breath we take,
A journey of wonder, never to break.

Boldly Standing Tall

Through the storms and through the rain,
I find my strength, I face the pain.
With head held high, I claim my space,
Boldly standing tall, I embrace my grace.

Roots run deep, I won't back down,
Like a sturdy oak, I wear my crown.
Each challenge faced, I learn to grow,
With steadfast heart, my spirit will glow.

Voices may doubt, but I will not sway,
For in my heart, I know the way.
Fearless I walk, on this path divine,
Boldly standing tall, my dreams align.

The world may twist, it may bend and break,
But I will rise, for my soul's own sake.
With courage afire, I'll make my call,
With unwavering strength, I stand tall.

The Sky of My Aspirations

Above the clouds, my dreams take flight,
Soaring high in the brilliant light.
Each star a goal, a vision so clear,
In the sky of aspirations, I persevere.

Winds may howl, the storms may rage,
But I'm the author of my own page.
With wings of hope, I'll rise once more,
To dance with the sky, to explore.

Every dawn brings a chance anew,
Painting the heavens in hues so true.
In the canvas of blue, my passions ignite,
Guiding me forward, like the stars at night.

For in this vast and endless dome,
I've found a place I can call home.
The sky of my aspirations, wide and free,
A limitless realm where I choose to be.

A Heart Like a Mountain

In silence it stands, so proud and tall,
Whispers of strength in the air do call.
Covered in snow, with peaks so grand,
A heart like a mountain, forever to stand.

Through storms it weathers, unbending, bold,
Stories of courage in whispers told.
Roots deep in the earth, a timeless grace,
A heart like a mountain, a sacred place.

With valleys rich, life finds its way,
Sunrise to sunset, a dance each day.
In shadows it casts, a shelter for all,
A heart like a mountain, answering the call.

As seasons do change, it remains the same,
Mighty and still, without seeking fame.
A testament of nature, steadfast and free,
A heart like a mountain, true legacy.

The Echo of My Confidence

From depths within the voice does rise,
In echoes sweet, beneath the skies.
A melody bold, a spark, a light,
The echo of my confidence, taking flight.

In moments of doubt, it soars like a song,
A chorus of strength, where I belong.
Resonating loud, through valleys and peaks,
The echo of my confidence, the heart speaks.

Each challenge I face, it calls me near,
A whispered promise, a void to clear.
In stillness I find, its rhythm and rhyme,
The echo of my confidence, through space and time.

With every step taken, its power grows,
A force unyielding, a truth that flows.
In every heartbeat, in every glance,
The echo of my confidence, my dance.

Swelling Like the Tide

In moonlit glow, the water sways,
A dance of nature, in rhythmic plays.
With each rise and fall, the ocean breathes,
Swelling like the tide, as the heart believes.

Gentle waves kiss the sandy shore,
Whispers of secrets, a timeless lore.
With every surge, it finds its stride,
Swelling like the tide, with change as a guide.

In storms it rages, a furious flight,
Yet calms to peace in the soft twilight.
Nature's embrace, both wild and wide,
Swelling like the tide, with nothing to hide.

A cycle eternal, with ebb and flow,
Lessons of patience in each undertow.
With love's embrace, it won't collide,
Swelling like the tide, with the heart as its guide.

Wings of the Unfurling Dawn

As night yields softly to morning's grace,
A tender light begins to trace.
With colors bold, the sky does yawn,
Wings of the unfurling dawn.

In every hue, a promise sings,
The hope that each new journey brings.
A gentle breeze, a fragrant lawn,
Wings of the unfurling dawn.

With whispers sweet of dreams anew,
Awakening hearts to skies so blue.
In every moment, a new world drawn,
Wings of the unfurling dawn.

So spread your arms and greet the light,
Let go of shadows, embrace the flight.
In every heartbeat, grace is shown,
Wings of the unfurling dawn.

The Pinnacle of Self

In the mirror, a face I find,
Reflecting truths, so well defined.
Climbing high with every breath,
Embracing life, defying death.

With every step, I claim my fate,
Shattering chains I shall negate.
The summit glows, a guiding star,
I reach for dreams that seem too far.

Voices whisper from the past,
Echoes linger, hoping to last.
In the silence, I hear my heart,
A melody that sparks new art.

United with the strength within,
The battle lost, the war to win.
At the pinnacle, I stand bold,
A story woven, bright and gold.

Winds of a Giant's Dream

Across the hills, the breezes sway,
Carrying whispers of yesterday.
A giant's dream takes flight and flies,
Kissing the stars in midnight skies.

Mountains rise to greet the gales,
Stories echo in ancient trails.
With every gust, a chance to soar,
Boundless realms to explore once more.

Fragments of hopes in every breeze,
Entwined in leaves of timeless trees.
Harness the winds, let passions glide,
On the crest of dreams, let us ride.

Together we'll weave a tapestry,
Painted with love, wild and free.
In the winds, let our laughter beam,
Together we find the giant's dream.

The Dawn of My Valor

Morning light breaks through the gloom,
Chasing away the shadows' doom.
With rising sun, my spirit beams,
Awakening the bravest dreams.

Each step forward, a battle won,
Champion of fate, I'll not be shunned.
In the dawn, my courage swells,
I rise to conquer, fate compels.

Heart ignited, unyielding fire,
Ready to climb, to reach higher.
With every moment, I embrace
The valor blooming in this space.

In the light of this new day,
I'll forge a path, come what may.
For within me burns the essence bright,
The dawn of valor in full flight.

Whispering Heights of Grandeur

Amidst the clouds, the silence reigns,
Echoes of greatness in my veins.
From heights where eagles dare to soar,
The world unfolds, a vibrant shore.

Each whisper carries tales untold,
Secrets of glory, brave and bold.
With every heartbeat, mountains sway,
In grandeur's arms, I long to stay.

Stars align to guide my way,
Lighting paths where shadows play.
In this realm of peace, I find,
The whispers beckon, souls entwined.

Atop the peaks, my spirit thrives,
In wondrous heights, my heart arrives.
Embracing life, with joy I soar,
Whispering heights, forevermore.

The Surge of Inner Giants

Awakening whispers rise and flow,
From depths where silent power grows.
A flicker of strength stirs the heart,
Each pulse ignites a brand-new start.

Beneath the weight of fear we stand,
With courage we move, hand in hand.
The giants we hold, deep in our core,
Unleashing dreams we can't ignore.

A roar of purpose fills the night,
Guiding us toward the light.
Each step a bold declaration made,
In the face of doubt, we won't fade.

Together we rise, fierce and free,
Embracing the strength of you and me.
The surge within cannot be tamed,
For the giants we've nurtured are now unchained.

Rivers of Radiance

In the gentle flow of twilight's hue,
Rivers spark as dreams come true.
Reflecting light in whispered tones,
They carry hope to hearts unknown.

The dance of waters, bright and bold,
Tales of deliverance, softly told.
Each ripple sings of joy and grace,
Carving paths in time and space.

From mountain high to valleys low,
Their current shapes the seeds we sow.
In currents swift, our worries shed,
Among these waters, spirits fed.

Embracing starlight, each flow a kiss,
In rivers of radiance, find your bliss.
Let the luminescence guide your way,
As night turns bright and melds with day.

The Giant Within

Hidden within, a giant sleeps,
In quiet shadows, its power creeps.
Strength cloaked in a gentle guise,
Awakening dreams that rise and rise.

With each heartbeat, a courage grows,
Unleashing force no one yet knows.
Running rivers of grit and fire,
The giant stirs, igniting desire.

In the stillness, we find our might,
With the giant's roar, we claim our light.
No longer bound by fear's cruel chain,
For within us lies a vast domain.

As shadows fade, we stand our ground,
With every whisper, the giant's found.
Embrace the surge, let life begin,
For true strength lies in the giant within.

In Shadows of Greatness

In shadows deep, where giants dwell,
Secrets of wisdom cast a spell.
Among the echoes of ages past,
Greatness thrives, shadows are cast.

Each footstep we take unearths the past,
In silence, our courage is amassed.
Beneath the weight of whispers low,
The seeds of greatness begin to grow.

Lifted by dreams that burn so bright,
In the shadows, we find our light.
Beneath the surface, hope takes flight,
With every heartbeat, we ignite.

Embrace the darkness, let it teach,
A path of greatness lies in reach.
In shadows, our potential unfurls,
For within us lies a world of pearls.

A Symphony of Giants

In the heart of the forest, great giants stand tall,
They whisper of ages, their stories enthrall.
With roots deep and wide, they cradle the ground,
In their shade, ancient wisdom is found.

Leaves dance to the rhythm of a soft, gentle breeze,
Nature's own music, a sweet symphony frees.
Echoes of laughter resound through the trees,
A harmony woven in nature's decrees.

Each branch tells a tale, each twig holds a dream,
Life's fragile threads intertwine like a seam.
Together they flourish, unyielding, serene,
In the chorus of giants, a world unforeseen.

From the depths of the silence, their spirits arise,
A testament to time beneath sweeping skies.
In the symphony sung, both powerful and kind,
The giants remind us of what we can find.

Boundless in My Being

In the mirror of stars, I find my own light,
Boundless and free, I take flight in the night.
With dreams intertwined like the threads of my soul,
I journey through shadows, I strive to be whole.

The whispers of nature call out to my heart,
Each breath a reminder that I play a part.
In the vastness of silence, my spirit unfolds,
With courage unchained, my destiny molds.

I dance with the winds, I swim with the tides,
In the ebb and the flow, my passion abides.
Each moment a canvas, my life a bold chance,
To paint my own story in the art of romance.

Though mountains may rise and the oceans may roar,
Boundless in spirit, I reach for much more.
With every heartbeat, I chase my true calling,
In the depths of existence, my soul keeps on sprawling.

Walking Amongst Titans

In a world of giants, I tread with awe,
Each step is a blessing, each breath a raw law.
Amongst their shadows, I seek my own place,
Feeling their power, I chase after grace.

The ground trembles softly beneath titanic feet,
Reverberations of wisdom in their heartbeat.
With each whispered secret, they gift me their strength,
I learn from their presence, in breadth and in length.

In awe of their stature, I find my own rise,
Like a seed in the soil, I strive for the skies.
With roots interwoven, in unity grow,
Together we flourish, in the sun's golden glow.

Walking amongst titans, I gather my worth,
In communion with giants, I cherish this earth.
Their stories, they echo, in the depths of my mind,
A journey of courage, together we find.

Shadows of My Lofty Ambition

In the twilight's embrace, my dreams take their flight,
Shadows stretch long, fading into the night.
With hopes like stars, I reach for the sky,
Each heartbeat a whisper, as time passes by.

Mountains loom high, yet my spirit feels bold,
With visions of futures that shimmer like gold.
In the depths of my heart, ambition ignites,
Guiding me forward, through treacherous nights.

The path may be winding, but I'll never sway,
For shadows of starlight will light up the way.
With courage as fuel, I ascend to my dreams,
In the dance of ambition, the universe beams.

With every step taken, I'm carving my fate,
In shadows of greatness, I'll never be late.
For dreams may be distant, like whispers in wind,
But with passion and patience, I strive to ascend.

Steps Towards Eternity

With every step, the path unfolds,
Whispers of time, their stories told.
Under the stars, where dreams align,
Each moment lost, yet feels divine.

The shadows dance, the light will wane,
In quiet solace, we bear the strain.
A journey deep, where echoes sway,
Forever seeking, yet led astray.

In every breath, a heartbeat's quake,
The promise of dawn, a chance to wake.
In the fading dusk, we find our grace,
In the twilight's glow, a sacred space.

Steps towards a realm where time stands still,
Guided by dreams and a guiding will.
In the vast unknown, we tread so bold,
Towards eternity, our fates unfold.

Portrait of a Behemoth

In shadows cast by ancient trees,
A figure stirs, with strength and ease.
With eyes that gleam like distant stars,
A titan born of tales from afar.

Its roar resounds through valley deep,
Awakening dreams from silent sleep.
A creature forged in nature's might,
A guardian of the endless night.

Upon its back, the world does sway,
Mountains bow to its sovereign play.
In every breath, the tempest rumbles,
Echoing deep as the earth tumbles.

Yet beneath the weight, a heart so true,
In its embrace, life does renew.
This behemoth, fierce and grand,
Holds the essence of this land.

The Allure of Immensity

In the vast expanse where horizons blend,
Whispers of secrets that nature lends.
Mountains rise like giants from the sea,
Their peaks crowned in clouds, wild and free.

The oceans stretch, a boundless sway,
Mirroring skies in a dance of gray.
Waves crashing softly on golden sand,
A promise of beauty, ever unplanned.

Under the stars, the cosmos gleams,
Holding the weight of our wildest dreams.
The allure of space, a siren's call,
Enchanting hearts, inviting all.

In every corner, the vastness we seek,
In the quiet hush, our spirits speak.
Embracing the grand, we savor the view,
The allure of immensity, forever true.

Cascading Into Greatness

Like waterfalls that plunge from high,
A journey starts, beneath the sky.
Each drop a challenge, fierce and bold,
Flowing with courage, a tale unfold.

Through rocky paths and narrow bends,
The stream of life, it twists and bends.
With every splash, something ignites,
Transforming shadows into lights.

The mountains stand, a witness proud,
To dreams that rise, to hearts unbowed.
In the rush, we find our fate,
Cascading forward, we elevate.

Within each twist, potential waits,
Sharp turns may lead to open gates.
As we cascade, we embrace the flight,
Into greatness, we take our height.

Milton Keynes UK
Ingram Content Group UK Ltd.
UKHW030751121124
451094UK00013B/789

9 789916 908334